MALMBERG

Home Maths Ages 8–9

Anita Straker

CAMBRIDGE
UNIVERSITY PRESS

1

Ask an adult to time you.

You need pencil and paper. Write only the answers.

1 60 – 7.

2 15×100.

3 Take 65p from £5.

4 45 + 8.

5 How many fours in 32?

6 5 + 8 + 5 + 1.

7 One third of 30.

8 $8 \times 5 \div 4$.

9 How many millilitres in 3 litres?

10 What is next: 495, 497, 499, □ ?

11 How many days in 5 weeks?

12 Round 127 to the nearest 10.

13 Increase 70 by 60.

14 □ – 23 = 12.

2

Hot air balloons

Do this on your own.

You need pencil and paper.

These hot air balloons are labelled with four-digit counting numbers.

Use the digits 0, 3, 5 and 8 to make four-digit counting numbers,

In each number each digit must be different.

You can label 18 different balloons.

List the numbers on the balloons in order, largest first.

Understand place val
Order four-digit numb

3

Witches

Play this with a partner.

W	I	T	C	H	E	S
1	2	3	4	5	6	7

Each letter has a value.

Add up the numbers in the words below.

Your partner should check and say if you are right.

1 IT

2 WE

3 HIT

4 WET

5 SEW

6 SIT

7 WITH

8 TEST

9 ITCH

10 THESE

11 CHEWS

12 CHEST

Think of more words using the letters of WITCHES.

Ask your partner to work out what they are worth.

You must say if your partner is right.

dd several small numbers
se addition facts to 20

4

Threes

Two, three or four people can play.

You need two dice.

Each player needs pencil and paper.

Each player should draw a grid like this.

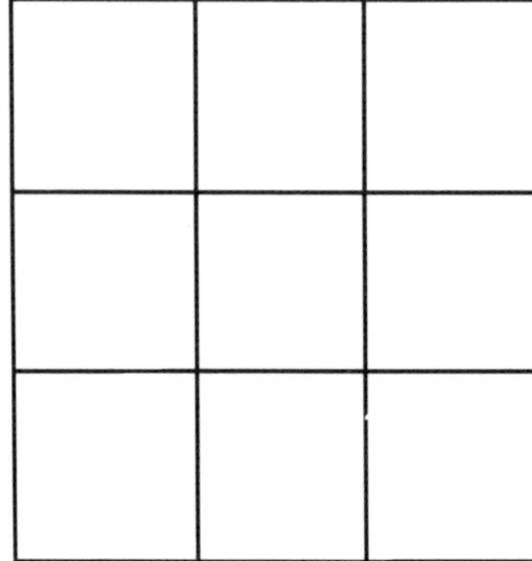

Take turns to roll the two dice. Each spot is worth 3.

Write your score on your grid.

Carry on until your grid is full of numbers.

Now take turns to roll the dice again.

If your score is the same as a number on the grid, cross it out.

Otherwise wait for your next turn.

The first to cross out all their numbers wins.

Change the rules

Make each spot worth 4, 5 or 6.

Practise times-tables (3, 4, 5,

5

Ask an adult to read you these.

You need pencil and paper. Write only the answers.

1 37 times 10.

2 120 minus 80.

3 Double 45.

4 Add 30 to 58.

5 Take £3.70 from £10.

6 32 divided by 4.

7 100 take away 66.

8 How many grams in 7 kilograms?

9 Decrease 48 by 6.

10 Write in figures **six hundred and five**.

11 How many 2p coins in 50p?

12 One quarter of 16.

13 How long is it from 9:50 a.m. to noon?

14 Find the product of 13 and 3.

6

Targets

Do this on your own.

You need pencil and paper.

Use two of these numbers each time.

Copy and complete these.

1. ... + ... = **42**
2. ... − ... = **18**
3. ... + ... = **36**
4. ... − ... = **8**
5. ... + ... = **27**
6. ... − ... = **7**
7. ... + ... = **43**
8. ... − ... = **2**
9. ... + ... = **60**
10. ... − ... = **15**

d and subtract pairs of two-digit numbers
rk out a strategy

7

First to 100

Play with a partner.

Share a pencil and paper.

Start with 50.

Take turns.

Choose any number from 6 to 9.

Add it to the previous total and write it on the paper.

The winner is the player to reach **exactly** 100.

Play several times.

Now start at 150.

Take turns to subtract any number from 6 to 9.

The winner is the player to reach **exactly** 100.

Add or subtract 6, 7, 8 or 9 to a two-digit number

8

Ask an adult to time you.

You need pencil and paper. Write only the answers.

1 $\frac{1}{3}$ of 24.

2 700 + 800.

3 One half of 29.

4 $2 \times 10 \div 4$.

5 $\square + 15 = 31$.

6 $27 \div 3$.

7 70 – 8.

8 Roughly, what is 68 + 83?

9 Write 12 metres in centimetres.

10 6 + 1 + 9 + 2.

11 Round 456 to the nearest 100.

12 Find the product of 20 and 4.

13 How long is it from 8:20 p.m. to midnight?

14 What is next: 36, 39, 42, $\square$?

9

20 up

Two, three or four people can play.

You need two dice.

Each player needs pencil and paper.

Each player should draw a grid like this.

8	9	10	11
12	13	13	14
15	16	17	18

Take turns to roll the two dice.

Add the two numbers to find the total.

Take the total from 20.

Cross out the answer on your grid.

If there is no new number to cross out, score 3 points.

Stop when the first player has crossed out all their numbers.

The winner is the player with the fewest points.

Change the rules

Add 5 to each number on the grid when you draw it and take the total from 25.

10

Money bags

Two, three or four people can play.

You need pencil and paper for each player, and a dice.

Each player should draw a big purse like this.

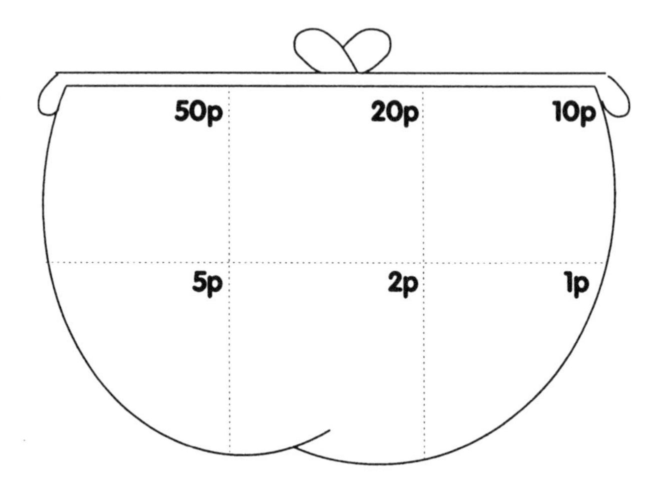

Take turns to roll the dice.

The dice tells you how many of a coin you have won.

Choose a space in your purse and write how much you have won.

For example, if you throw 4 and choose the 2p space, you win four 2p coins, and write 8p in the space.

Each space can be used only once.

When all the spaces are full, find the total in your purse.

The winner is the player with the most in their purse.

Play several times.

Change the rules

Make the 1p space a £1 space, and the 2p space a £5 space.

Find multiples of coin values and their total sum
Understand the relative values and work out a strate

11

Countdown

Two, three or four people can play.
You need a dice.
Each player needs pencil and paper.

Each player starts with a total of 100.
Take turns to roll the dice.
If you roll, say, 3 your score can be 30 or 3.
Subtract your score from your previous total.

Have seven turns each.
If you go below zero you are out.
The winner is the player whose final total is closest to zero.

Play several times.

derstand place value
btract a single digit or a multiple of 10

12

Ask an adult to read these to you.
You need pencil and paper. Write only the answers.

1 90 multiplied by 3.
2 97 take away 60.
3 Double 132.
4 How many fours in 24?
5 Decrease 62 by 5.
6 One half of 150.
7 Take 28p from 50p.
8 Find the total of 80p and £4.70.
9 Find the difference between 97 and 130.
10 How many minutes in 3 hours?
11 What must you add to 36 to make 60?
12 Round 507 to the nearest 10.
13 How many 50p coins in £12.50?
14 What is next: 505, 507, 509, … ?

13

Ask an adult to time you.

You need pencil and paper. Write only the answers.

1. $3 \times 10 \div 5$.
2. $90 - 6$.
3. 6 times 4.
4. $3 + 5 + 4 + 7$.
5. Write 4004 in words.
6. Multiply 31 by 3.
7. $36 \div 4$.
8. One third of 18.
9. Write 6000 grams in kilograms.
10. $48 + \square = 102$.
11. How many 20p coins make £4?
12. Take £7.32 from £10.
13. 423×2.
14. What is missing: 25, 29, $\square$, 37 ?

14

Jimps

Do this on your own.

You need pencil and paper.

Meg made up a new maths word.

She said that a 'jimp' is a single digit, or a sign such as +, –, ×, ÷ or =.

She used 4 'jimps' to make 16.

This is how she did it.

Write 3 more ways of making 16 using 4 jimps.

Write 5 different ways of making 25 using 5 jimps.

Write 6 different ways of making 36 using 6 jimps.

Now ask an adult to check.

Use knowledge of number bonds and times-tabl
Think flexibly and work systematically

15

Race against time

Play with a partner who has a watch or clock with a second hand.

You need a pack of playing cards.

Use the ace to 10 of each suit.

Shuffle the cards.

Put them face down in a pile.

Your partner should say 'Go' and time you.

Turn over the top card.

Say four times the number.

If your partner says you are right, keep the card.

If not, put the card back at the bottom of the pile.

Carry on until you have won all the cards.

When you win the last card say 'Stop'.

How many minutes and seconds did you take?

Play again. Can you beat your record?

Change the rules

a. Say 3 times the number.

b. Say 6 times the number.

'actise times-tables (3, 4, 6)
me minutes and seconds

16

Products

Do this with a partner.

Share a pencil and paper.

Draw this grid.

6	8	9	10	12
15	16	18	20	21
24	25	27	28	30
32	35	36	40	45

Take turns to choose any two numbers and say them.

They can be the same or different.

Multiply them together.

If the answer is on the grid, mark it with your initial.

If not, wait for your next turn.

Each number on the grid can be marked only once.

Carry on until each number on the grid is marked.

The winner is the one with most initials on the grid.

Change the rules

a. Choose 3 numbers to multiply, instead of 2.

b. Add the numbers instead of multiplying them.

Identify factors and calculate product
Work out a strategy

17

Ask an adult to read you these.
You need pencil and paper. Write only the answers.

1 45 divided by 5.

2 87 plus 5.

3 40 add 68.

4 Take £3.15 from £5.

5 Multiply 22 by 4.

6 Nine fours.

7 Double 235.

8 Write 2000 millilitres in litres.

9 What is the cost of 3 tickets at £4.99 each?

10 How many seconds in 2½ minutes?

11 Find the total of £2.50 and £3.75.

12 One quarter of 28.

13 What is next: 478, 488, 498, ... ?

14 How many millimetres in 1 centimetre?

18

Know when to stop

Two, three or four people can play.
You need a dice.
Each player needs pencil and paper.

Take turns to roll the dice as many times as you like.
Add the numbers you roll in your head to get your score.
Choose when to end your turn.
Beware – if you roll a 6 your score for that turn is wiped out!

Add your score to your previous total and write it on your paper.
The first to get to 60 wins.

ep a running total of small numbers
ıd pairs of two-digit numbers

19

Pet weight

Do this on your own.

You need pencil and paper.

You are able to balance your dog using one or more of these weights.

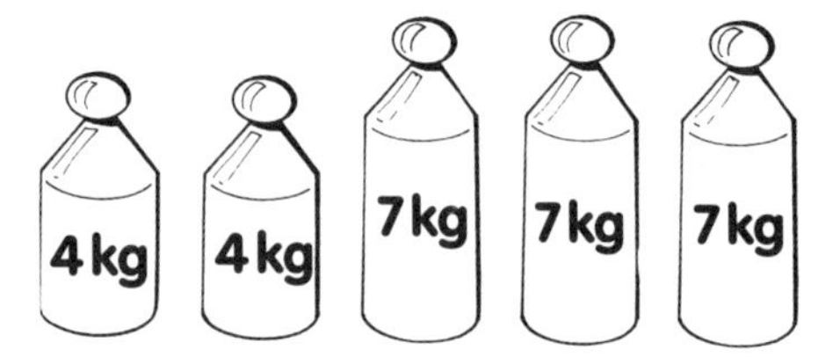

How heavy is your dog?

There are 11 different possibilities.

Write a list of them.

Change the rules

What if you had two 5 kg and three 9 kg weights?

Add weights in kilograms
Work systematically

20

Ask an adult to time you.
You need pencil and paper. Write only the answers.

1 $5 \times 2 \times 7$.

2 $2 + 3 + 8 + 4$.

3 52 minus 5.

4 9×50.

5 Take 23p from 50p.

6 ¼ of 32.

7 $72 + \square = 99$.

8 Two T-shirts at £5.95 each cost …?

9 Divide 63 by 3.

10 Write 7 centimetres in millimetres.

11 Round 449 to the nearest 100.

12 12×0.

13 $260 \div 10$.

14 Roughly, what is 705 – 287?

21

Please be nice!

Four people should play.

You need a dice.

Share a pencil and paper.

Draw this on your paper.

Write your names on the left.

Mum			
Gran			
Ben			
Me			

Take turns to roll the dice.

Write the number in an empty box.

You can write in your own line of boxes or in someone else's.

Carry on until each box has a digit in it.

The winner is the one with the biggest three-digit number next to their name.

Play four times.

Take turns to go first.

Change the rules

a. The winner has the smallest number next to their name.

b. Draw a grid with four columns and make four-digit numbers.

nderstand place value in three-digit numbers
'ork out a strategy

22

Network

Two, three or four people can play.

You need a 5p coin.

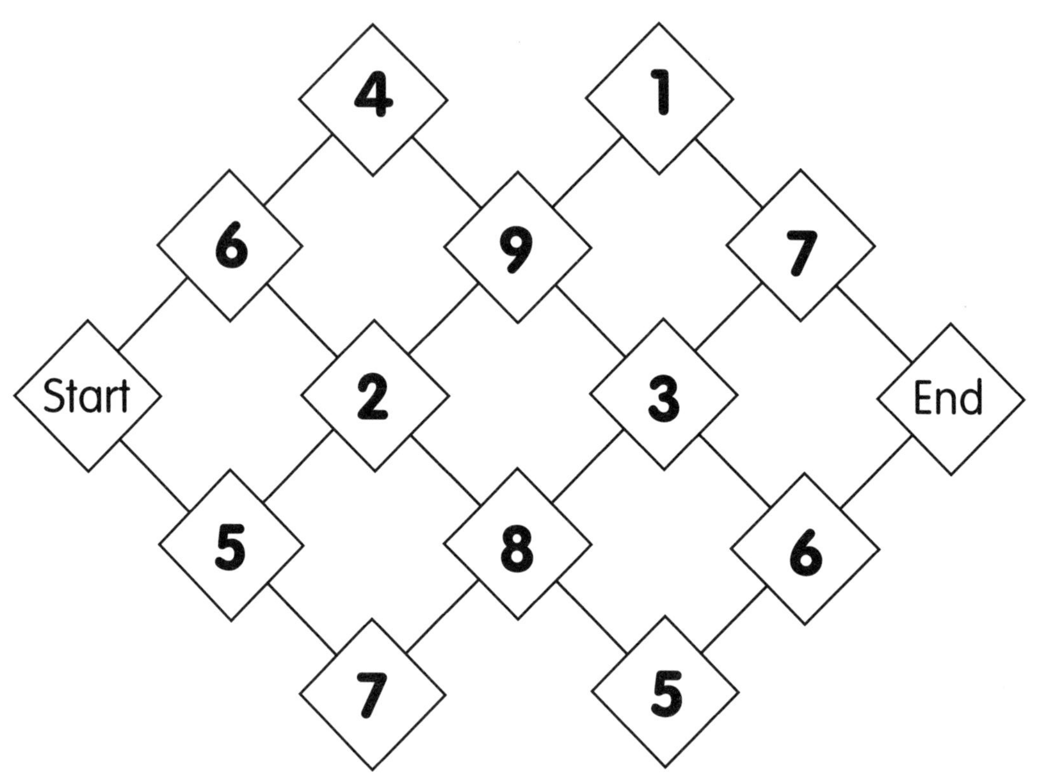

The first player chooses a target number between 20 and 70.

Take turns to push the coin **along the lines** from 'Start' to 'End'.

Keep a running total of the numbers you go through.

You can go through a number more than once.

The player who gets nearest to the target wins that round.

Play several times.

Take turns to go first

Add several small numbers
Think logically to eliminate what won't wo

Home Maths Ages 8–9 Answers

1

1. 53
2. 1500
3. £4.35
4. 53
5. 8
6. 19
7. 10
8. 10
9. 3000 millilitres (3000 ml)
10. 501
11. 35 days
12. 130
13. 130
14. 35

2

The balloons are numbered as follows:

8530	5830	3850
8503	5803	3805
8350	5380	3580
8305	5308	3508
8053	5083	3085
8035	5038	3058

3

1	IT	5
2	WE	7
3	HIT	10
4	WET	10
5	SEW	14
6	SIT	12
7	WITH	11
8	TEST	19
9	ITCH	14
10	THESE	27
11	CHEWS	23
12	CHEST	25

More words: HE, HIS, SEE, THE, SHE, WISE, STEW, HISS, STITCH ...

5

1. 370
2. 40
3. 90
4. 88
5. £6.30
6. 8
7. 34
8. 7000 grams (or 7000 g)
9. 42
10. 605
11. 25
12. 4
13. 2 hours 10 minutes
14. 39

6

1. 8 + 34 = 42
2. 26 – 8 = 18
3. 17 + 19 = 36
4. 34 – 26 = 8
5. 8 + 19 = 27
6. 26 – 19 = 7
7. 26 + 17 = 43
8. 19 – 17 = 2
9. 34 + 26 = 60
10. 34 – 19 = 15

8

1. 8
2. 1500
3. 14.5 or 14½
4. 5
5. 16
6. 9
7. 62
8. 150
9. 1200 centimetres (1200 cm)
10. 18
11. 500
12. 80
13. 3 hours 40 minutes
14. 45

12

1. 270
2. 37
3. 264
4. 6
5. 57
6. 75
7. 22p
8. £5.50
9. 33
10. 180 minutes
11. 24
12. 510
13. 25
14. 511

13

1. 6
2. 84
3. 24
4. 19
5. four thousand and four
6. 93
7. 9
8. 6
9. 6 kilograms (or 6 kg)
10. 54
11. 20
12. £2.68
13. 846
14. 33

14

Examples of ways of making 16 with 3 jimps

8 + 8 =	8 x 2 =
9 + 7 =	4 x 4 =

making 25 with 5 jimps

25 x 1 =	30 – 5 =
50 ÷ 2 =	75 ÷ 3 =
20 + 5 =	19 + 6 =

making 36 with 6 jimps

2 x 3 x 6 =	144 ÷ 4 =
50 – 14 =	20 + 16 =
86 – 50 =	5 x 6 + 6 =

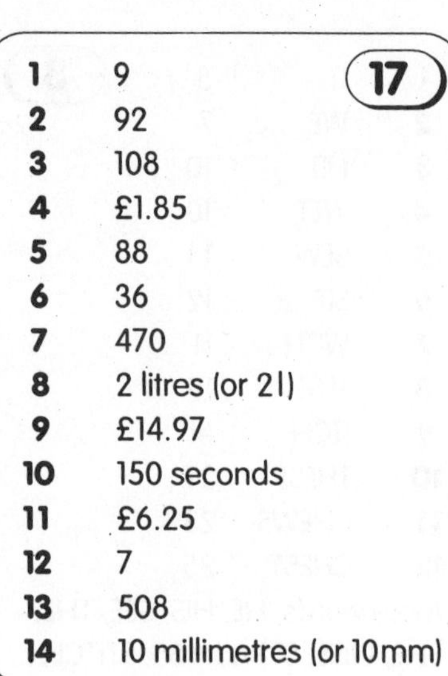

17

1	9
2	92
3	108
4	£1.85
5	88
6	36
7	470
8	2 litres (or 2 l)
9	£14.97
10	150 seconds
11	£6.25
12	7
13	508
14	10 millimetres (or 10 mm)

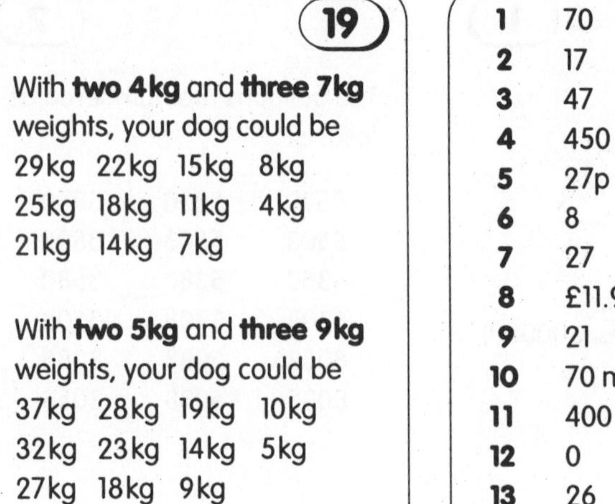

19

With **two 4kg** and **three 7kg** weights, your dog could be

29kg 22kg 15kg 8kg
25kg 18kg 11kg 4kg
21kg 14kg 7kg

With **two 5kg** and **three 9kg** weights, your dog could be

37kg 28kg 19kg 10kg
32kg 23kg 14kg 5kg
27kg 18kg 9kg

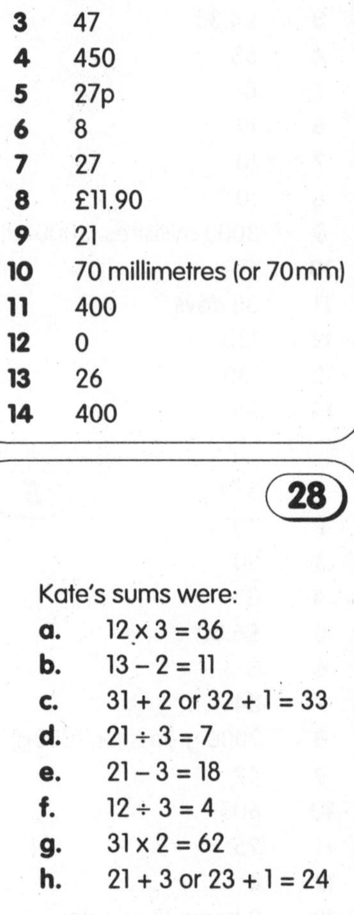

20

1	70
2	17
3	47
4	450
5	27p
6	8
7	27
8	£11.90
9	21
10	70 millimetres (or 70 mm)
11	400
12	0
13	26
14	400

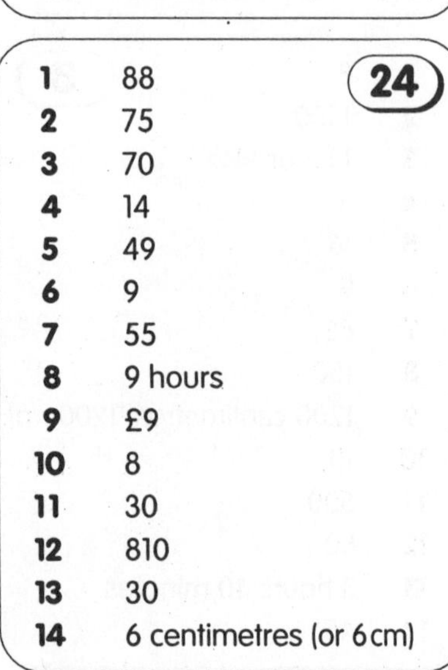

24

1	88
2	75
3	70
4	14
5	49
6	9
7	55
8	9 hours
9	£9
10	8
11	30
12	810
13	30
14	6 centimetres (or 6 cm)

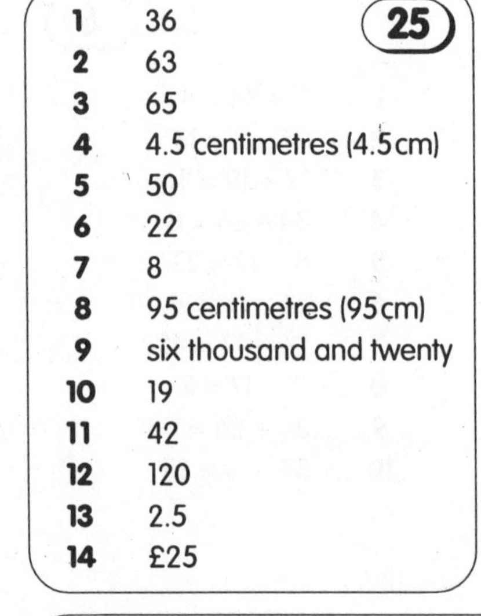

25

1	36
2	63
3	65
4	4.5 centimetres (4.5 cm)
5	50
6	22
7	8
8	95 centimetres (95 cm)
9	six thousand and twenty
10	19
11	42
12	120
13	2.5
14	£25

28

Kate's sums were:

a. 12 x 3 = 36
b. 13 – 2 = 11
c. 31 + 2 or 32 + 1 = 33
d. 21 ÷ 3 = 7
e. 21 – 3 = 18
f. 12 ÷ 3 = 4
g. 31 x 2 = 62
h. 21 + 3 or 23 + 1 = 24

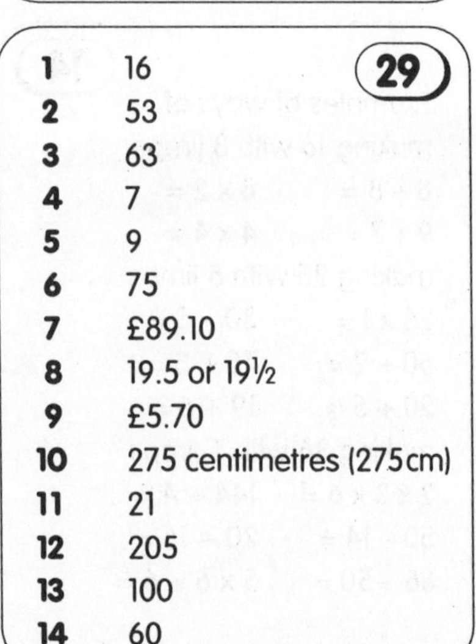

29

1	16
2	53
3	63
4	7
5	9
6	75
7	£89.10
8	19.5 or 19½
9	£5.70
10	275 centimetres (275 cm)
11	21
12	205
13	100
14	60

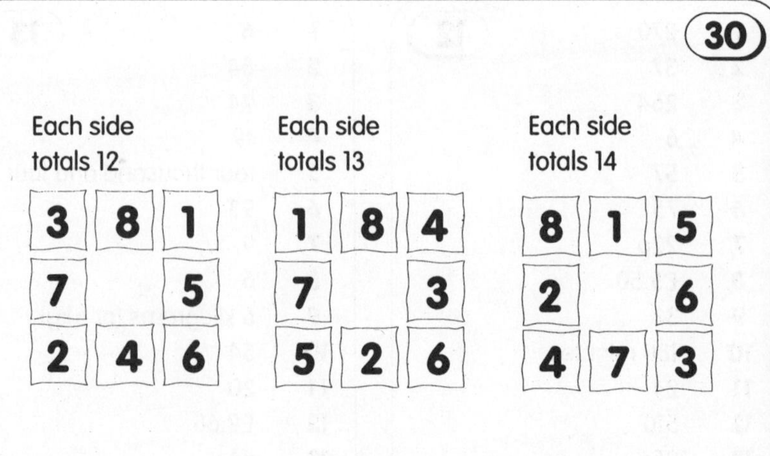

30

Each side totals 12

3	8	1
7		5
2	4	6

Each side totals 13

1	8	4
7		3
5	2	6

Each side totals 14

8	1	5
2		6
4	7	3

31

For example,

1	$2 \times 3 - 4 - 1$	11	$13 + 2 - 4$	21	$24 \times 1 - 3$	31	$34 - 2 - 1$
2	$1 + 2 + 3 - 4$	12	$2 \times 4 + 3 + 1$	22	$21 + 4 - 3$	32	$12 \times 3 - 4$
3	$1 \times 4 + 2 - 3$	13	$12 + 4 - 3$	23	$2 \times 3 \times 4 - 1$	33	$31 + 4 - 2$
4	$3 + 4 - 1 - 2$	14	$21 - 4 - 3$	24	$1 \times 2 \times 3 \times 4$	34	$(13 + 4) \times 2$
5	$12 - 3 - 4$	15	$13 + 4 - 2$	25	$2 \times 3 \times 4 + 1$	35	$32 + 4 - 1$
6	$1 + 3 + 4 - 2$	16	$34 \div 2 - 1$	26	$23 + 4 - 1$	36	$41 - 2 - 3$
7	$13 - 2 - 4$	17	$34 \times 1 \div 2$	27	$32 - 4 - 1$	37	$32 + 4 + 1$
8	$2 + 3 + 4 - 1$	18	$23 - 1 - 4$	28	$23 + 4 + 1$	38	$42 - 3 - 1$
9	$23 - 14$	19	$12 + 3 + 4$	29	$31 + 2 - 4$	39	$42 \times 1 - 3$
10	$1 + 2 + 3 + 4$	20	$23 + 1 - 4$	30	$13 \times 2 + 4$	40	$42 - 3 + 1$

32

1 32
2 600
3 8
4 12
5 262
6 0.1
7 28
8 390
9 43
10 100
11 799
12 60
13 68 millimetres (68 mm)
14 450

33

1 Most change 80p
Least change 5p

2 6 possibilities:
£1.95
£2.25
£2.40
£2.85
£3.15
£3.60

3 **£2.60**
New baby
Happy New Year
Birthday

£2.90
New baby
Happy New Year
Thank you

35

Two pin knock-downs

a. 23 15, 8
b. 26 15, 11
c. 21 13, 8

Three pin knock-downs

a. 31 7, 11, 13
b. 34 8, 11, 15
c. 26 7, 8, 11

Four pin knock-downs:
the 5 possibilities are
39, 41, 43, 46, 47

36

1 180
2 37
3 43
4 58
5 459
6 25
7 54
8 75 millimetres (or 75 mm)
9 7
10 £15.80
11 1000
12 500
13 6
14 266, 268, 270, 272, 274

37

1 92
2 27
3 163
4 6 millimetres (6 mm)
5 400
6 $3/10$
7 80
8 198
9 seven thousand and ten
10 60
11 26
12 3.5 metres (or 3.5 m)
13 £17.70
14 0.75

39

1	8	AS, SIN
2	7	IN, TIT
3	5	IT
4	9	AT, TIN
5	11	AN
6	16	NAG, AIR
7	17	RAN, GAG
8	15	ART, TAR, RAT, NAN
9	13	TAN, GAS
10	10	TAG, RIG
11	21	RAY
12	18	RAG

More words: SIT, SAG, TINT, RING, GNAT, STIR, STRING …

40

Slices in fruit salads:

1 2 apple
4 banana
3 orange

2 3 apple
1 banana
3 orange

3 4 apple
2 banana
2 orange

4 1 apple
3 banana
2 orange

41

1	14
2	46
3	3.6
4	71
5	$\frac{1}{4}$
6	20
7	74
8	£9.95
9	£40.30
10	246
11	$1\frac{1}{4}$
12	500
13	34
14	3000 centimetres (3000 cm)

42

To find how to score 30 with three doubles, find how to score 15 with three singles.

Double each of these:

1, 1, 13	2, 2, 11	3, 5, 7
1, 2, 12	2, 3, 10	3, 6, 6
1, 3, 11	2, 4, 9	4, 4, 7
1, 4, 10	2, 5, 8	4, 5, 6
1, 5, 9	2, 6, 7	5, 5, 5
1, 6, 8	3, 3, 9	
1, 7, 7	3, 4, 8	

43

1 13 + 29 + 31 = 73

2 13 + 15 + 29 = 57

3 24 + 29 + 31 = 84

4 13 + 24 + 31 = 68

5 13 + 15 + 24 = 52

6 13 + 15 + 31 = 59

44

1	48
2	83
3	27
4	0.7
5	18
6	4
7	75
8	1.7 cm or 17 mm
9	131, 133, 135, 137, 139
10	£9.96
11	800
12	48 months
13	34
14	70 centimetres (or 70 cm)

23

Say it!

Two or three people can play.

You need two dice and some dried beans.

Take turns to roll both dice.

Make a two-digit number.

If you roll, say, 5 and 4 you can make 54 or 45.

Try to make a number that divides exactly by 3, 4, 5 or 6.

For example, if you made 45 you could say '45 is a multiple of 5'.

If the other players agree you are right you win a bean.

If you cannot do it you must wait for your next turn.

The first to win 12 beans wins the game.

Recognise multiples of 3, 4, 5 or 6

24

Ask an adult to read you these.

You need pencil and paper. Write only the answers.

1 92 minus 4.

2 7.5 times 10.

3 Divide 140 by 2.

4 Add 4, 3 and 7.

5 Halve 98.

6 One third of 27.

7 105 subtract 50.

8 How long is it from 6:00 p.m. to 3:00 a.m?

9 Find the total of £6.80 and £2.20.

10 How many threes in 24?

11 300 divided by 10.

12 Round 809 to the nearest 10.

13 How many 20p coins make £6?

14 Write 60 millimetres in centimetres.

25

Ask an adult to time you.
You need pencil and paper. Write only the answers.

1 2 times 3 times 6.

2 37 + □ = 100.

3 26 + 39.

4 Write 45mm in centimetres.

5 43 + 7.

6 Divide 66 by 3.

7 40 ÷ 5.

8 Take 5 centimetres from 1 metre.

9 Write 6020 in words.

10 Half of 38.

11 What is next: 24, 30, 36, □ ?

12 Find the product of 40 and 3.

13 One tenth of 25.

14 Roughly, what is £10.86 + £14.17?

26

Take from 20

Two, three or four people can play.
You need a pack of playing cards.
Use the ace to 10 of each suit.

Shuffle the cards and put them face down in a pile.
Turn over two cards.
The first to say the total of the two cards takes the pair.
The winner is the one who gets the most pairs.

Change the rules

The first to say how many more to make 20 wins the pair.

Practise instant recall of addition and subtraction fa

Tables

Learn your 6 times-table by heart.

Say it forwards.

Say it backwards.

Make up a tune and sing it.

Say it in a funny voice. Can you make people laugh?

Ask an adult to ask you questions like:

Eight sixes.
9 times 6.
6 multiplied by 4.
How many sixes in 30?
Divide 42 by 6.
Divide 6 into 54.
Share 36 equally among 6.

Now it is your turn to make up questions for your partner.
You must say if they are right. Here are some to start with.

What is 6 multiplied by itself?
What number multiplied by 6 equals 18?
What number divided by 6 equals 7?
What must I divide 24 by to get 6?
What is the product of 6 and 9?
What is the remainder when you divide 32 by 6?

Change the rules

a. Do the 3 times-table.

b. Do the 4 times-tables.

Learn by heart the 3, 4 and 6 times-tables

28

Disaster!

Try these by yourself.

You need pencil and paper.

There's been a disaster!

Kate's dog Ben went out in the rain.

When he came in he shook himself like mad.

Water splashed all over Kate's homework.

Can you help her do it again?

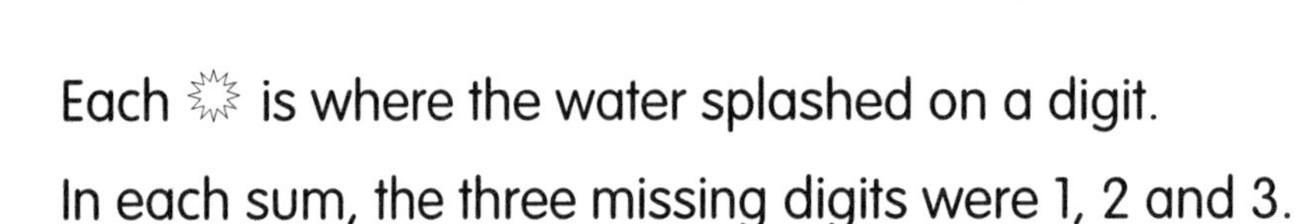

Each ✹ is where the water splashed on a digit.

In each sum, the three missing digits were 1, 2 and 3.

Can you copy and complete these?

a. ✹✹ × ✹ = 36

b. ✹✹ − ✹ = 11

c. ✹✹ + ✹ = 33

d. ✹✹ ÷ ✹ = 7

e. ✹✹ − ✹ = 18

f. ✹✹ ÷ ✹ = 4

g. ✹✹ × ✹ = 62

h. ✹✹ + ✹ = 24

Use knowledge of number facts and times-tables
Think logically to eliminate what won't work

29

Ask an adult to read you these.

You need pencil and paper. Write only the answers.

1 8 multiplied by 2.

2 100 minus 47.

3 Increase 54 by 9.

4 700 divided by 100.

5 One quarter of 36.

6 56 plus 19.

7 Take 90p from £90.

8 Halve 39.

9 6 pens at 95p each cost … ?

10 Write 2.75 metres in centimetres.

11 Divide 4 into 84.

12 5 times 41.

13 Roughly, what is 395 divided by 4.

14 One third of 180.

30

Squares

Do this on your own.

You need a piece of paper, a pencil and some scissors.

Use the paper to make 8 number cards.

1	2	3	4	5	6	7	8

Arrange your cards in a square shape.

Make each side of the square add up to 12.

Change the rules

a. Each side must total 13.

b. Each side must total 14.

Add three small numbers to total 12, 13 or 14.
Think logically to eliminate what won't work

31

One, two, three, four

Two, three or four people can play.

You each need pencil and paper.

1 2 3 4

Each player should write a list of numbers 1 to 40.

Someone says 'Go'.

Everyone tries to make each of the numbers on their list.

For each number, use each of the digits 1, 2, 3, 4 but only once each.

For example, you could make 26, because $26 = 23 + 4 - 1$.

You can use any operation ($+$, $-$, $\times$ or $\div$).

Write your calculation next to each number.

The player who has made the most numbers after 15 minutes wins.

Use knowledge of number facts and times-tables
Think logically to eliminate what won't work

32

Ask an adult to time you.

You need pencil and paper. Write only the answers.

1 Eight fours.

2 Roughly, what is 59×9?

3 $75 + \square = 83$.

4 $4 \times 6 \div 2$.

5 Add 8 to 254.

6 Write $\frac{1}{10}$ as a decimal.

7 Half of 56.

8 Round 392 to the nearest 10.

9 $92 - 49$.

10 $1000 \div 10$.

11 What is next: 805, 803, 801, $\square$?

12 15 times 4.

13 Write 6.8 centimetres in millimetres.

14 4.5×100.

33

Greetings

Do this by yourself.

You need pencil and paper.

1 You can spend up to £3 on three different greetings cards.
What is the most change you could get?
What is the least change you could get?

2 How much is a packet of 3 cards that are all the same?
There are 6 possibilities.
Can you write them all?

3 A packet of 3 different cards costs £2.60.
Which cards are in it?
What if the packet costs £2.90?

Ask an adult to check your answers.

Find money totals and work out change
Work systematically

Find the time

Start off with someone to help.

You need pencil and paper, and a watch with a second hand.

Your partner should tell you when to start.

Close your eyes.

Open them when you think 30 seconds have gone by.

How close were you?

Practise until you are close.

Now time these yourself. Write each answer.

1 How long can you stand on one foot, without holding on?

2 How many times in 15 seconds can you touch your knees and then your shoulders?

3 How many times in one minute can you write '**one thousand**'?

4 How long does it take you to read two pages of your book?

5 How long does it take you to brush your teeth properly?

6 How long does it take to put on your socks and shoes and do them up?

7 How long does the toaster take to toast a slice of bread?

8 How long does it take for the kettle to boil?

Estimate 30 seconds
Practise timing in minutes and seconds

35

Bowling

Try this by yourself.

You need pencil and paper.

1 Which 2 pins must you knock down to score these?

a. 23 **b.** 26 **c.** 21

2 Which 3 pins must you knock down to score these?

a. 31 **b.** 34 **c.** 26

3 What scores can you get if you knock down 4 pins?

There are 5 possibilities. Try to write them all.

Add two, three or four numbers up to 20
Think logically to eliminate what won't work

36

Ask an adult to read you these.
You need pencil and paper. Write only the answers.

1 6 times 30.

2 Halve 74.

3 81 minus 38.

4 Double 29.

5 Decrease 468 by 9.

6 One quarter of 100.

7 18 plus 36.

8 How many millimetres is 7.5 centimetres?

9 How many fours in 28?

10 What is the cost of 4 cakes at £3.95 each?

11 Round 962 to the nearest 100.

12 5000 divided by 10.

13 Find the difference between 57 and 63.

14 Write all the even numbers between 265 and 275.

37

Ask an adult to time you.

You need pencil and paper. Write only the answers.

1 $37 + 55$.

2 Half of 54.

3 $170 - 7$.

4 Take 4 mm from 1 cm.

5 Roughly, what is 19×19?

6 Write 0.3 as a fraction.

7 $8000 \div 100$.

8 206 subtract 8.

9 Write 7010 in words.

10 Find the product of 4, 3 and 5.

11 $\square \times 2 = 52$.

12 Write 350 cm in metres.

13 3 books at £5.90 each cost ...?

14 Write $\frac{3}{4}$ as a decimal.

38

What's left?

Two, three or four people can play.

You need pencil and paper to keep the score, a dice and a pack of cards.

Use the ace to six of each suit.

Shuffle the cards. Put them face down in a pile.

Take turns. Roll the dice – a 1 counts as 10.

Draw two cards and make a two-digit number.

With, say, 3 and 6 you can make 36 or 63.

Divide your two-digit number by the number you rolled.

The remainder is your score for that round.

Beware – the remainder might be zero!

The winner is the first to get a total score of 30.

Divide two-digit numbers by 2, 3, 4, 5, 6 or 10.
Find the remainders and add them up.

Sting ray

Ask all your family to join in.

Add up the numbers standing for the letters.

Find some two-letter or three-letter words that are worth these.

1	8	**5**	11	**9**	13
2	7	**6**	16	**10**	14
3	5	**7**	17	**11**	21
4	9	**8**	15	**12**	18

Secretly make a longer word using the letters of STING RAY.

Work out what it is worth and tell everyone.

Can they guess what your word is?

dd several small numbers
se addition facts to 20

40

Fruit salad

Ask an adult to help you get ready to do this.

Wash your hands before you begin.

You need four saucers, a knife and a chopping board.

You need a peeled apple, orange and banana.

Cut 10 apple slices, 10 orange slices and 10 banana slices.

Put out four saucers. Make a different fruit salad in each one.

1 This salad has:

2 slices of apple;

twice as many banana slices as apple slices;

9 slices of fruit altogether.

2 This salad has:

the same number of orange slices as apple slices;

two less banana slices than apple slices;

7 slices of fruit altogether.

3 This salad has:

8 slices of fruit altogether;

half of the slices are apple;

one quarter of the slices are orange.

4 This salad has:

3 times as many banana slices as apple slices;

1 more orange slice than apple slices;

6 slices of fruit altogether.

Have you used all your fruit slices? Now you can eat your fruit salad!

Use addition facts to 20
Think logically

41

Ask an adult to read you these.
You need pencil and paper. Write only the answers.

1 90 minus 76.
2 Halve 92.
3 36 divided by 10.
4 Add 28 and 43.
5 Write 0.25 as a fraction.
6 100 divided by 5.
7 Double 37.
8 Find the cost of 5 balls at £1.99 each.
9 Write 4030 pence in pounds.
10 Find the product of 6 and 41.
11 Add one half to three quarters.
12 Approximately, what is 9 times 49?
13 Find the difference between 81 and 47.
14 Write 30m in centimetres.

42

Darts

Do this by yourself.
You need pencil and paper.

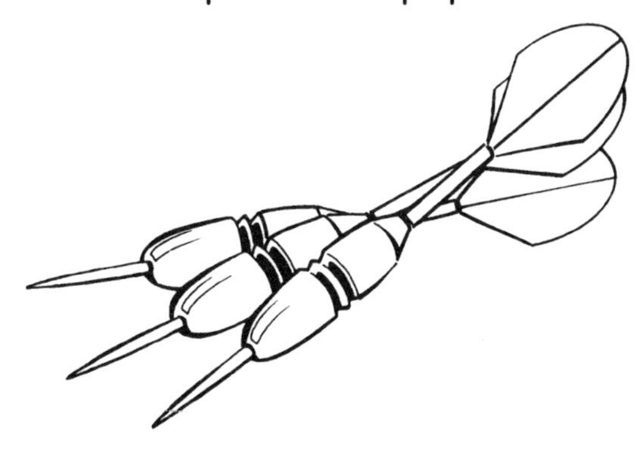

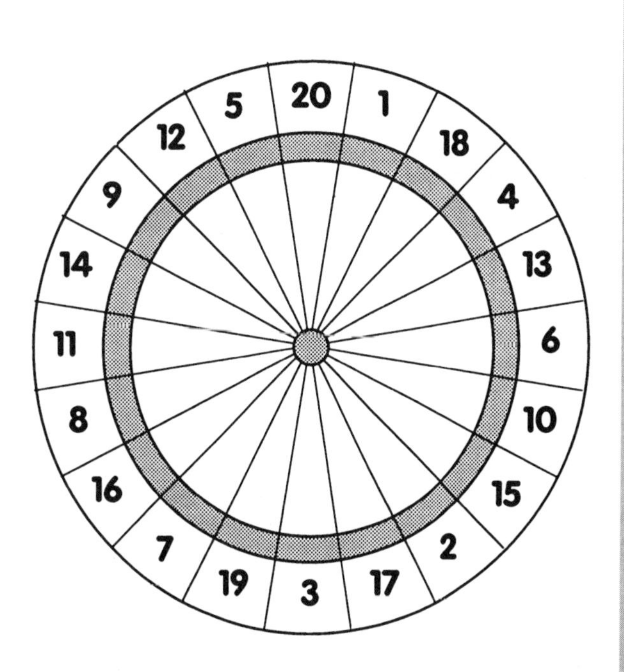

You score 30 with three doubles.
There are 19 different ways to do it.
How many can you find?

ouble and add small numbers
ink logically and work systematically

43

More targets

Do this on your own.

You need pencil and paper.

Each time, use three different numbers from this set.

Copy and complete these.

1. ... **+** ... **+** ... **= 73**
2. ... **+** ... **+** ... **= 57**
3. ... **+** ... **+** ... **= 84**
4. ... **+** ... **+** ... **= 68**
5. ... **+** ... **+** ... **= 52**
6. ... **+** ... **+** ... **= 59**

Add three two-digit numbers
Work out a strategy

44

Ask an adult to time you.
You need pencil and paper. Write only the answers.

1 □ × 2 = 96.

2 36 + 47.

3 80 – 53.

4 Write $\frac{7}{10}$ as a decimal.

5 6 × 6 ÷ 2.

6 100 divided by 25.

7 15 multiplied by 5.

8 Take 3 millimetres from 2 centimetres.

9 Write all the odd numbers between 130 and 140.

10 4 tapes at £2.49 each cost ...?

11 Round 798 to the nearest 10.

12 How many months in 4 years?

13 Find the difference between 92 and 58.

14 Write 700 millimetres in centimetres.

45

Differences

Two, three or four people can play.

You need a pack of playing cards.

Use the ace to 9 of each suit.

Each player needs pencil and paper.

Shuffle the cards.

Deal everyone 2 cards face up.

Each player uses their cards to make two two-digit numbers.

With, say, 4 and 1 you would make 14 and 41.

Find the difference between your two numbers.

Do this in your head.

Write the difference on your paper.

The player who has the smallest difference scores a point for that round.

Return the cards to the pack.

Shuffle them and deal again.

The winner is the player with most points after 10 rounds.

Change the rules

The winner is the player who gets the least number of points.

btract a pair of two-digit numbers
nderrstand place value

PUBLISHED BY THE PRESS SYNDICATE OF THE UNIVERSITY OF CAMBRIDGE
The Pitt Building, Trumpington Street, Cambridge CB2 1RP, United Kingdom

CAMBRIDGE UNIVERSITY PRESS
The Edinburgh Building, Cambridge CB2 2RU, United Kingdom
40 West 20th Street, New York, NY 10011-4211, USA
10 Stamford Road, Oakleigh, Melbourne 3166, Australia

First published 1998

Printed in the United Kingdom by Scotprint Ltd, Musselburgh

A catalogue record for this book is available from the British Library

ISBN 0 521 655536 paperback

Cover Illustration by Graham Round
Cartoons by Tim Sell